Keto Diet Cookbook

The Official Keto Diet Recipes

<u>Liam Miles</u>

Keto Diet Recipes

Mary Coley

Table of Contents

can be in any fashion deemed liable for any hardship or damages that may befall them after undertaking information described herein.

Additionally, the information in the following pages is intended only for informational purposes and should thus be thought of as universal. As befitting its nature, it is presented without assurance regarding its prolonged validity or interim quality. Trademarks that are mentioned are done without written consent and can in no way be considered an endorsement from the trademark holder.

INTRODUCTION

The **ketogenic diet** is a very low carbohydrate diet that turns the body into a fat-burning machine. It has many proven benefits for weight loss, health and performance, as millions of people, have experienced.

So, if you're looking for that, stay here because we're going to talk about everything that involves this super diet!

What is the Ketogenic Diet?

A ketogenic diet is well known for being a **low carbohydrate diet**, where the body produces ketone bodies in the liver to be used for energy. Ketone bodies are water-soluble fatty acid molecules that replace glucose as fuel for the body.

When you eat something high in carbohydrates, your body makes glucose and insulin.

- Glucose is the easiest molecule for your body to convert and use as energy, i.e., it is chosen as a priority before any other energy fuel.

- The **insulin** is produced for processing glucose into the bloodstream, making it around the body.

As glucose is being used as a primary energy, its **fats** are not needed and therefore are **stored**. Typically, in a normal, more carbohydrate-rich diet, the body will use **glucose as the main form of energy**. By decreasing carbohydrate intake, the body is induced into a state known as ketosis.

Ketosis is a natural process that the body goes through to help us survive when we don't eat enough. Ketone bodies are formed in this state as a result of the breakdown of fats in the liver.

The ultimate goal of a properly ketogenic diet is to force your body into this metabolic state.

Our bodies are incredibly adaptable to what you put into them - when you eat a diet rich in good quality fats and eliminate carbohydrates, it will begin to **burn those stored fats as its main source of energy**.

Benefits of Ketogenic Diet

There are numerous benefits of a ketogenic diet. Among them are weight loss and increased energy levels. Most people can safely benefit from a diet low in carbohydrates and fat.

Below, you will find a shortlist of the benefits you can receive from a ketogenic diet:

Mental Focus Many people use the ketogenic diet specifically to increase mental performance. That's because ketone bodies are an excellent source of fuel for the brain. When you lower your carbohydrate intake, you avoid big spikes in blood sugar. Thus resulting in better focus and concentration. Studies show that a good intake of fatty acids can have impactful benefits for our brain function.

1. **Weight Loss**

Because the ketogenic diet relies on your body fat for energy, there are obvious weight-loss benefits. Insulin (the fat-storing hormone) levels drop dramatically, transforming your body into a fat-burning powerhouse.

Scientifically, the ketogenic diet showed better results compared to diets with low fat and carbohydrates, even in the long run. Many people seeking this often incorporate coconut oil into their diet (increases the production of ketone bodies and fat loss), especially when taken with coffee in the morning.

3. Energy Increase

By giving your body a better, more reliable energy source, you'll feel more energized throughout the day. Fats are the most effective molecules to use as metabolic fuel. In addition, fat has the power to increase satiety and ends up leaving us "full" for longer.

1. **Decreases Acne**

It is common for a ketogenic diet to show great improvements in the skin. Proof of this is a study that shows decreases in skin lesions and inflammation when switching to a low-carb diet. Another study also shows a likely connection between carbohydrate intake and increased acne, so it's very likely that a ketogenic diet can help with this issue as well.

1. **Controls blood sugar**

Because of the meals consumed, the ketogenic diet naturally reduces blood sugar levels. In comparison to low-calorie diets, studies demonstrate that the ketogenic diet is a more effective strategy to control and prevent diabetes. If you have type 2 diabetes or are pre-diabetic, a ketogenic diet should be seriously considered.

1. **Improves cholesterol**

Low-carbohydrate and high-fat diets show a dramatic increase in HDL (good cholesterol) and a decrease in the concentration of LDL (bad cholesterol) particles when compared to low-fat diets.

Ketogenic Diet Foods

Contrary to what many people think, a ketogenic diet can be very tasty, with recipes - which we will bring here - delicious and best of all if you go hungry because fats provide great satiety.

It's a good idea to have a plan in place before beginning a ketogenic diet. This entails having a workable diet plan on hand. What you consume is determined by how quickly you want to enter a ketogenic state.

The lower your carbohydrate intake (less than 15 grams per day), the faster you'll reach ketosis, a condition of better performance and fat burning.

A very low carbohydrate intake is recommended, with carbohydrates coming primarily from vegetables, nuts, and dairy products when available.

Refined carbohydrates, including wheat (bread, pasta, cereals), starch (potatoes, beans, veggies), and high-glycemic-index fruits, are not recommended. Avocado, star fruit, strawberry, kiwi fruit, and lemon, among other fruits that can be ingested in moderation, are modest exceptions.

Do not eat on the ketogenic diet.

- **Grains** - Wheat, corn, rice, cereals, etc.

- **Sugar** - honey, agave, demerara sugar, coconut sugar, corn syrup, brown sugar, etc.

- **Fruits** - apples, bananas, grapes, oranges, etc.

- **Tubers** - potatoes, yams, cassava, etc.

What to eat on the ketogenic diet

- **Meat** - fish, beef, lamb, poultry, etc.

- **Green leaves** - spinach, kale, etc.

- **Vegetables** - Broccoli, cauliflower, carrots, beets, pumpkin, etc.

- **Dairy products** - ghee butter, lactose-free whole yoghurt, lactose-free cheeses, etc.

- **Oilseeds** - cashew nut, nut, baru, macadamia, hazelnut, sunflower seed, etc.

- **Fruits** - avocado, raspberry, blueberry, blackberry, lemon, strawberry, kiwi, etc.

- **Sweeteners** - stevia, erythritol xylitol

- **Other Fats** - coconut oil, olive oil, avocado oil, etc.

What to drink on the ketogenic diet

- **Water** - at least 2 litres a day

- **Tea** - moringa, chamomile, mint, hibiscus, lemon balm, etc.

- **Coffee**

- **SuperCoffee** - optimized version of regular coffee, containing very high-quality fats, thermogenic spices, protein and all this in a practical and instant version

- **Red Wine** - does not present any major problems if ingested occasionally and in a dose of 1 glass

SURF & TURF

INGREDIENTS

- ✓ 360 g beef fillets
- ✓ 8 king prawns
- ✓ 2 vine tomatoes
- ✓ Salt
- ✓ 1 REWE regional shallots
- ✓ 3 toe (s) of garlic
- ✓ 2 tbsp butter
- ✓ pepper
- ✓ 1 pinch (s) of sugar
- ✓ 200 g green beans
- ✓ 1 sprig (s) of savory
- ✓ 2 tbsp clarified butter
- ✓ 2 branch (e) thyme
- ✓ Cayenne pepper
- ✓ 0.5 bunch of chives

PREPARATION

Take beef fillets (approx. 180 g each) from the refrigerator. Pulp the prawns and remove the intestines. Score the tomato skin and put in boiling salted water for 10 second blanch

Immediately peel off the skin, quarter, core and cut into small cubes. Peel and finely dice shallot and 1 clove of garlic. Heat 1 tablespoon of butter in a small pan. Sauté shallot and garlic. Add tomatoes and season with salt, pepper and sugar.

Clean the beans and blanch them until they are firm to the bite in boiling salted water. Drain and add the tomatoes. Wash the savory, shake dry, chop finely and add to the beans

Heat clarified butter in a pan, beef fillets with 1 clove of garlic pressed on and thyme on both sides

to sear STH

and then let it rest for 10 minutes. Meanwhile, fry the prawns in clarified butter with 1 pressed clove of garlic and season with salt, pepper and cayenne pepper. Wash the chives, shake dry, cut into fine rings and add to the prawns. Season the steaks with salt and pepper, serve with prawns and vegetables.

ENTRECÔTE (RIB EYE STEAK)

INGREDIENTS

- ✓ 2 entrecôte steaks
- ✓ 2 tbsp vegetable oil
- ✓ Sea-salt
- ✓ freshly ground pepper

PREPARATION

Wash the meat and pat dry. Heat the cast iron pan or grill pan and add the oil. When the oil is hot, sear the meat on both sides for about 2 minutes.

Continue cooking in the preheated oven at 130 ° C for approx. 5-10 minutes, the core temperature of the meat should be approx. 54 ° C.

Take out, season with salt and pepper on both sides and cover and let rest for approx. 4 minutes.

CAULIFLOWER TALER WITH HERB QUARK

INGREDIENTS

- ✓ 400 g cauliflower
- ✓ 150 g parmesan cheese
- ✓ 2 eggs (M)
- ✓ 1 pinch (s) of pepper
- ✓ 1 pinch (s) of salt
- ✓ 1 pinch (s) of nutmeg
- ✓ 400 g quark
- ✓ 100 ml milk
- ✓ 15 g chives
- ✓ 15 g parsley

- ✓ *15 g cress*

- ✓ *15 g dill*

- ✓ *Pinch of herbal salt*

PREPARATION

Preheat the oven to 200 ° C top and bottom heat. Wash cauliflower and grate finely. Alternatively, chop in a blender, but do not puree. Coarsely grate the parmesan. Mix the cauliflower, parmesan, eggs and spices (pepper, salt, nutmeg) well in a large bowl.

Shape the cauliflower mixture into 6 thalers. Line the baking sheet with parchment paper and place the thalers on it. Bake in the oven for 20-25 minutes until golden brown.

Wash the herbs and chop them into small pieces. Mix with quark and milk in a bowl and season with herb salt and pepper.

CAULIFLOWER PUREE WITH TURKEY BREAST FILLET AND LAMB'S LETTUCE

INGREDIENTS

- ✓ 500 g cauliflower
- ✓ 50 ml of cream
- ✓ 1 tbsp butter
- ✓ Pinch of nutmeg
- ✓ 0.5 tsp salt
- ✓ 2 turkey fillets

- ✓ 0.5 tsp paprika sweet

- ✓ 0.5 tsp paprika rose sharply

- ✓ 2 tbsp rapeseed oil

- ✓ 100 g lamb's lettuce

- ✓ 1 shallot

- ✓ 2 tbsp apple cider vinegar

- ✓ 3 tbsp olive oil

- ✓ Pepper (fresh)

PREPARATION

Wash the cauliflower and cut into small pieces. Then cook in salted water for 20 minutes. Meanwhile, wash and pluck the lettuce. Peel the shallot and cut into fine cubes. Put both in a salad bowl.

Season the turkey breast fillets with paprika, pepper and salt. Heat the rapeseed oil in a pan, fry the turkey breast fillets vigorously and then fry for 5-6 minutes on each side over a medium heat.

Drain the cauliflower and pound it finely with a potato masher. If necessary, puree a little finer with a hand blender. Add the butter, cream and nutmeg and stir the mixture with a whisk until creamy.

Dress the salad with apple cider vinegar, olive oil, pepper and salt. Serve with turkey breast fillet and cauliflower puree.

CAULIFLOWER GRATIN WITH HAM

INGREDIENTS

- ✓ 2 heads cauliflower (approx. 800 g each)

- ✓ Salt

- ✓ 250 g yes! Ham cubes

- ✓ 400 g yes! Whipped cream

- ✓ Pepper

- ✓ Grated nutmeg

- ✓ 120 g yes! Gouda Holland young in one piece

✓ 3 stalk (s) of chervil

✓ 100 g Sliced almonds

PREPARATION

Clean and wash the cauliflower and cut out the stalk. Pre-cook the cauliflower one after the other in plenty of boiling salted water for 10-12 minutes.

Leave the ham cubes in a pan without fat for about 5 minutes until crispy. Pour in the cream, bring to the boil and remove from the stove. Season to taste with salt, pepper and nutmeg. Put cauliflower in a colander and drain.

Finely grate the cheese. Place the cauliflower in a small ovenproof dish. Spread the ham cream over it and sprinkle with cheese. Bake in a preheated oven (electric stove: 200 ° C / convection: 175 ° C / gas: see manufacturer) for about 20 minutes.

In the meantime, wash the chervil, shake dry and pluck the leaves from the stems. Roast the almonds in a pan without fat for about 4 minutes until golden brown. Take the cauliflower out of the oven. Garnish with flaked almonds and chervil.

TOMATO AND MOZZARELLA OMELETTE

INGREDIENTS

- ✓ 4 tomatoes

- ✓ 1 red onion

- ✓ 250 g mozzarella

- ✓ 15 g basil leaves

- ✓ 8 eggs

- ✓ 100 ml milk

- ✓ 1.5 teaspoons sweet paprika

- ✓ Salt

- ✓ Pepper

✓ 4 tbsp rapeseed oil

PREPARATION

Wash tomatoes and cut into cubes. Peel and chop the onion. Drain the mozzarella and chop it into pieces. Chop two thirds of the basil, set aside for decoration.

Whisk eggs with milk and season with paprika, salt and pepper and stir in the basil.

Preheat the oven. Heat 2 tablespoons of oil, sauté half of the onion. Put half of the tomatoes in the pan, sprinkle with half of the mozzarella and pour over half of the egg milk. Put the pan in the oven and bake for about 10 minutes.

Take the omelette out of the pan and keep it warm. Heat 2 tablespoons of oil and prepare the second omelette in the same way. Sprinkle with the remaining basil on top.

SIMPLE KETO BREAD FROM THE CUP

INGREDIENT

- ➢ 1 egg
- ➢ pinch of salt
- ➢ 1 tbsp butter
- ➢ 1/2 teaspoon baking powder
- ➢ 5 tbsp almond flour
- ➢ 1 teaspoon MCT powder

PREPARATION

Heat butter in a cup in the microwave for 15 seconds until it has melted.

Swirl the butter so that the rim of the cup is moistened.

Mix the almond flour, egg, baking powder, salt, and MCT powder with a fork to form a smooth batter.

Bake the dough in the cup in the microwave at maximum power for about 100-115 seconds.

Important: Let cool down for 2 minutes before cutting. Either toast or baked with cheese and herbs in the oven.

KETO RHUBARB MERINGUE TART

INGREDIENT

- 180 g almond flour
- 10 g bamboo flour
- 1 egg (size M)
- 80 g erythritol
- 125 g butter, room temperature
- For the rhubarb filling:
- 500 g rhubarb
- 50 g erythritol
- 1 teaspoon locust bean gum
- For the meringue:
- 50 ml of water
- 200 g erythritol
- 2 egg whites
- pinch of salt

PREPARATION

Preheat the oven to 175 ° C with a fan oven.

Mix all the ingredients for the batter in a bowl.

Then, use your hands to knead the dough into a firm mass.

Dust the dough sufficiently with bamboo flour and roll the dough out between two layers of cling film.

Now press the dough into the greased form and bake it for 8-10 minutes until it is lightly brown.

Peel the rhubarb and cut it into small pieces.

Put the rhubarb pieces with erythritol in a saucepan and let everything simmer for about 5 minutes.

Sprinkle the carob gum on the compote and stir well.

Spread the rhubarb compote on the base and bake the tart for another 30 minutes.

Mix the water with 150 g of the erythritol in a small saucepan and let it simmer.

As soon as the erythritol has dissolved, remove the syrup from the stove and let it cool down a little.

Beat the egg whites with a pinch of salt until they set.

Slowly mix in the rest of the erythritol and continue to beat until stiff.

Meanwhile, carefully mix the erythritol syrup into the egg white mixture and continue to beat until a firm and shiny meringue is formed.

Put the mixture in a piping bag and squirt small dots on the tart.

Lightly brown the meringue in the oven for about 5 minutes using the grill function.

KETO BOX CAKE WITH HEART

INGREDIENT

- ➤ 1 pack of Simply Keto cake mix
- ➤ 1 pack of Simply Keto Kuchenglück baking mix
- ➤ Red, sugar-free food coloring
- ➤ 1 pack of Simply Keto cake mix
- ➤ 1 pack of Simply Keto Kuchenglück baking mix
- ➤ For the chocolate icing:
- ➤ White Xucker Chocolate
- ➤ Red, sugar-free food coloring
- ➤ Chopped pistachios
- ➤ Nuts or berries of your choice

PREPARATION

Prepare the baking mixture with the food coloring mixed in according to the instructions on the package and bake.

Let the cake cool down well.

Take the cooled cake out of the mold, cut it into slices and use the cookie cutter to poke hearts out of each slice.

Mix the baking mixture according to the instructions on the package.

Pour 1/3 of the mixture into the cake tin.

Place the cut-out heart pieces in the middle.

Fill the cake pan with the rest of the cake mixture until the hearts are well covered and the cake pan is filled.

Bake the cake according to the instructions.

Then let the cake cool down well.

Melt the chocolate carefully. Mix in a few drops of food coloring as required.

Drizzle the melted chocolate over the cooled cake and decorate as needed.

KETO ASPARAGUS FETA SALAD

INGREDIENT

- ➢ 500 g green asparagus
- ➢ 150 g feta
- ➢ 40 g pine nuts (2 heaped tablespoons)
- ➢ 4 spring onions
- ➢ Some basil leaves
- ➢ 250 g strawberries
- ➢ Salt pepper
- ➢ Some butter to fry
- ➢ 1 tbsp MCT oil
- ➢ 1 tbsp melted coconut oil
- ➢ 1-2 teaspoons powder erythritol
- ➢ 1 teaspoon Paulikocht green stuff spice

➢ Salt pepper

PREPARATION

Cut the woody lower part of the asparagus and the remaining asparagus into small pieces.

Fry the asparagus in butter over medium heat, pour a dash of water into the pan so that the asparagus is briefly sautéed.

Likewise, fry the pine nuts in butter until they turn slightly golden.

Wash and dice the strawberries.

Place the asparagus, pine nuts, strawberries and basil leaves in a bowl.

Cut the spring onion into small rings and mix in.

Crumble the feta over it.

Mix all ingredients well and spread over the salad.

LOW-CARB STRAWBERRY-RHUBARB JAM

INGREDIENT

- ➢ 500 g strawberries
- ➢ 500 g rhubarb
- ➢ 1 pack of sugar-free Simply Keto Gelierzauber

PREPARATION

Chop strawberries and rhubarb and cook them until everything is nice and soft.

Now puree everything and add the entire contents of the gelation magic pack.

Stir everything well and let everything simmer for about 5 minutes.

Boil your jam jars well and fill them with the finished jam while it is still hot.

Screw it on, turn it around and let it set.

LOW-CARB FRUIT DOME TARTLETS

INGREDIENT

- ➢ 1/2 pack of keto cakes
- ➢ 200 g of water
- ➢ 3 sheets of gelatin
- ➢ 200 g cream
- ➢ 10 drops of Aqua Plus raspberry
- ➢ 25 g powder erythritol
- ➢ 250 g of water
- ➢ 6 sheets of gelatin
- ➢ 50 g fruit of your choice (kiwi, mango, grapes, strawberries, raspberries). Use berries for the keto variant
- ➢ 4 dessert rings and hemispherical silicone molds

PREPARATION

Mix half of the keto cake mix with water and place in a greased 22 cm springform pan or on a baking sheet.

Bake the dough for about 20 minutes at 175 ° C fan oven.

Then let cool down completely.

Cut out the bottom with dessert rings.

Soak gelatine in cold water.

Mix the cream with Aqua Plus and powder erythritol.

Squeeze out the soaked gelatine and heat briefly in a small saucepan or in the microwave.

Carefully stir the liquid gelatine into the cream in portions.

Let the cream layer sit briefly and spread it on the bases in the dessert rings, tablespoon at a time.

Chill the molds in the refrigerator while you prepare the domes.

Soak gelatine in cold water.

Cut the fruits into small pieces and distribute them in the silicone mold.

Squeeze out the soaked gelatine and heat briefly in a small saucepan or in the microwave.

Add water and mix with the soaked gelatin.

Spread the gelatine water in the silicone molds and also chill until they are firm.

Loosen the individual bottoms from the dessert rings.

Also remove the fruit domes from the molds and carefully tip them onto the layer of cream.

FRUITY LOW-CARB NICE CREAM

INGREDIENT

- ➢ 200 g mango
- ➢ 100 g banana
- ➢ 100 ml coconut milk
- ➢ 20 g powder erythritol

PREPARATION

Peel the fruit, cut into small pieces and freeze for 4 to 5 hours.

Put the frozen fruit pieces in a blender and puree.

Add the remaining ingredients and mix in.

Pour the nice cream into bowls and serve immediately.

BAKED KETO PORRIDGE

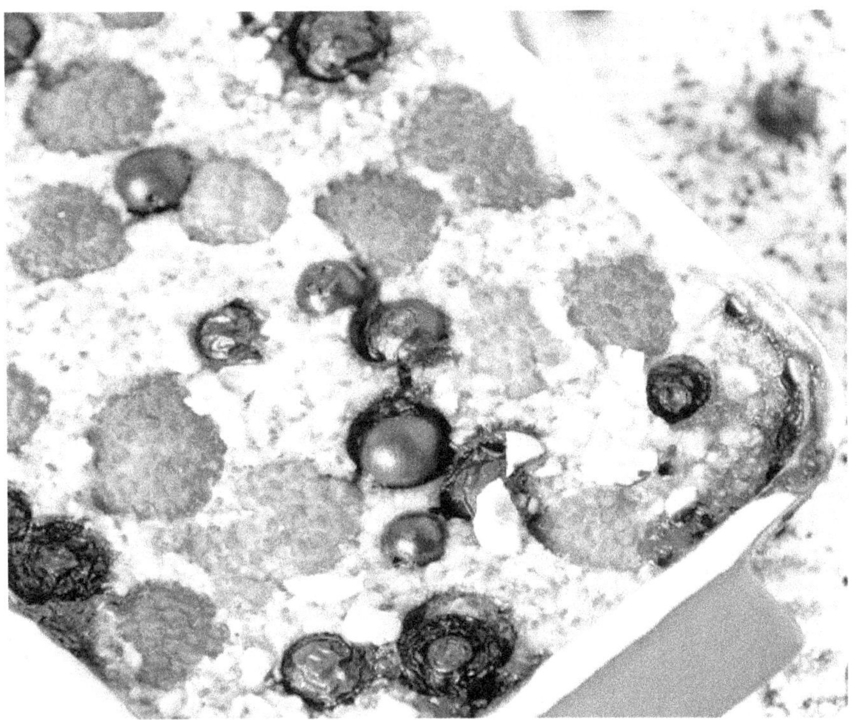

INGREDIENT

> - 130 g Simply Keto Porridge
> - 200 g unsweetened almond milk
> - 100 g berries at will

PREPARATION

Mix the porridge with the almond milk and pour the mixture into an ovenproof baking dish.

Spread the berries in it and press them a little into the mass.

Bake the porridge at 175 ° C for about 30 minutes until it is golden brown.

FILLED FRANKFURT WREATH - KETO

INGREDIENT

- 5 eggs
- 175 g erythritol
- 150 g butter
- 300 g ground almonds
- 40 g bamboo flour
- 1/4 teaspoon baking powder
- 270 g butter
- 270 g cream cheese
- 75 g powder erythritol
- 5 drops of vanilla flavor
- 100 g sugar-free strawberry fruit spread
- 50 g chopped hazelnuts
- 50 g erythritol gold preparation

PREPARATION

First, melt the butter.

Now put all the ingredients in a bowl and stir them until you have a homogeneous mass.

Now spread the dough in a greased bundt cake pan.

Now bake the cake for about 45 minutes at 170 ° C top / bottom heat (every oven is a bit different, so watch the cake after 60 minutes and take it out as soon as it starts to get dark).

Let the cake cool for 1 hour before removing it from the pan.

Beat the softened butter white with the mixer for at least 3 minutes.

Gradually add the powdered erythritol and keep stirring.

Finally add the remaining ingredients and stir them in.

Put the chopped hazelnuts and the erythritol gold in a small saucepan and melt the erythritol gold for about 3 minutes while stirring.

Then let the brittle cool completely and chop it up.

Cut the cooled cake twice horizontally and spread the strawberry fruit spread on the underside of the lower base.

Spread a quarter of the buttercream on the opposite cut surfaces and put the bottom back on top.

Do the same for the rest of the soil.

Brush the cake with the remaining buttercream and press the brittle around it.

Decorate the Frankfurt wreath with buttercream and fresh strawberries as you like.

KETO CHOCOLATE CHIP FRAPPUCCINO WITHOUT SUGAR

INGREDIENT

- ➤ 15 - 20 g Simply Keto drinking chocolate
- ➤ 60 ml espresso
- ➤ 250 ml unsweetened almond milk
- ➤ 250 g ice cubes
- ➤ 20 g cream
- ➤ Sugar-free chocolate drops
- ➤ 5 g coconut oil

PREPARATION

Prepare espresso and let it cool down. Put the drinking chocolate, the cold espresso, the unsweetened almond milk and the ice cubes in a blender and mix on a high level for about 30 seconds to a creamy mass. The ice cream can be in small, coarse pieces.

Melt the chocolate drops together with the coconut oil in a water bath and mix well.

Whip the cream until stiff.

Pour the frappuccino into a glass, top with the cream and drizzle the melted chocolate over it.

KETO LAHMACUN

INGREDIENT

- ➤ 1 pack of Simply Keto Pizza Mix

- ➤ 400 g of water

- ➤ 20 g of olive oil

- ➤ 250 g ground beef

- ➤ 1 white onion

- ➤ 1/2 bunch of parsley, finely chopped

- ➤ 1 pointed pepper

- ➤ 1 teaspoon tomato paste

- ➤ 1 clove of garlic

- ➢ 200 g chopped tomatoes from the can

- ➢ 1 teaspoon erythritol

- ➢ Oriental spices (cumin, oregano, paprika powder, chilli flakes) as desired

- ➢ Salt pepper

- ➢ 100 g feta cheese

- ➢ 1/2 romaine lettuce

- ➢ 1 small red onion

- ➢ 1 tomato

- ➢ 1/2 lemon

- ➢ 1/4 bunch of parsley

PREPARATION

Mix the baking mixture with water and olive oil and knead everything until a dough is formed.

Place parchment paper on the countertop and place half of the dough in the middle of it.

Roll out the dough long and thin between a layer of cling film.

Prick the dough several times with a fork, place it on a baking sheet and pre-bake it blind for 15 minutes at 200 ℃.

Do the same with the rest of the dough.

Peel off the onion and garlic and roughly chop them. Pluck the leaves from the parsley.

Chop the peppers too.

Put the onion & garlic pieces, the parsley leaves and the pepper pieces in a blender and blend them finely.

Put the ground beef in a mixing bowl and mix it with the chopped ingredients, tomato paste, and canned tomatoes.

Season the mince as you like and spread it thinly over the pre-baked dough.

Bake the lahmacun for another 10 minutes.

In the meantime, prepare the topping: Crumble the feta.

Cut the red onion into fine strips.

Dice the tomato.

Finely cut the lettuce.

Pluck the parsley leaves from the stems.

After baking, drizzle the lahmacun with a little lemon juice and top it with the prepared ingredients as desired.

KETO WAFFLES WITHOUT BAKING MIX

INGREDIENT

- ➢ 2 eggs
- ➢ 20 g erythritol
- ➢ 50 g ground almonds
- ➢ 1 teaspoon Baking powder
- ➢ 100 g cream cheese
- ➢ 1 pinch of salt

PREPARATION

Mix eggs and erythritol in a mixing bowl until frothy.

Add the remaining ingredients and mix everything into a homogeneous dough.

If necessary, rub the waffle iron with butter and add the dough by tablespoon.

Bake the waffle and top with powdered erythritol, cream and berries as desired.

CHOCOLATEY LOW-CARB COCONUT WAFERS WITHOUT A BAKING MIX

INGREDIENT

- ➢ 100 g ground almonds
- ➢ 2 eggs
- ➢ 20 g erythritol
- ➢ 25 g sugar-free dark chocolate drops
- ➢ 200 g desiccated coconut
- ➢ 200 ml coconut milk
- ➢ 50 g coconut oil
- ➢ 100 g erythritol
- ➢ 100g cream cheese
- ➢ 75 g Choco-Coco-Creme
- ➢ A square cake shapes

PREPARATION

Preheat the oven to 180 ° C fan-assisted.

Separate the egg yolks from the egg whites.

Gently melt the chocolate drops.

Mix the melted chocolate with ground almonds, erythritol and egg yolks.

Beat the separated egg whites until stiff and carefully fold them into the almond mixture.

Pour the dough into a square, greased or parchment-lined dish and bake for 20-25 minutes until the edges turn golden brown.

Let the base cool down well.

Mix the coconut milk with erythritol and cream cheese until the erythritol has completely dissolved.

Then add the coconut oil (it should be liquid, otherwise heat it up briefly) and the desiccated coconut.

Spread the mixture on the cake base and put it in the fridge for at least an hour.

Brush or sprinkle the cake with the chocolate and coco cream and cut it into small cubes.

SPRING-LIKE LOW-CARB ELDERBERRY TART WITH STRAWBERRIES

INGREDIENT

- 40 g almond flour
- 10 g gold flax flour
- 25 g ground almonds
- 20 g coconut flour
- 10 g baking cocoa
- 40 g erythritol
- 30 g coconut oil
- 50 g of water
- For the cream:
- 100 g white sugar-free chocolate
- 200 g cream cheese
- 150 g whipped cream
- 30 drops of Aqua Plus elderflower aroma

> ➤ 3 sheets of gelatin
> ➤ Fresh strawberries

PREPARATION

Preheat the oven to 175 ° C with a fan oven.

Mix all the ingredients for the batter in a bowl.

Use your hands to knead the dough into a solid mass.

Dust the dough sufficiently with bamboo flour and roll it out between two layers of cling film.

Now press the dough into the greased form, prick it several times with a fork and bake it for 8-10 minutes until it is lightly brown.

Then let cool down completely.

Heat the cream cheese and whipped cream in a small saucepan on medium heat and add the white chocolate drops.

Let the chocolate melt and stir everything into a homogeneous mass.

Soak the gelatin in cold water for about 5 minutes.

Then drain the gelatine and add it to the pot along with the Aqua Plus elderflower.

Stir thoroughly so that the gelatin dissolves evenly and pour the mixture into the cooled cake tin.

Put the tart in the cold for at least 2 hours and decorate it with fresh strawberries before serving.

KETO PASTEL DE NATA - PORTUGUESE CUSTARD TARTS

INGREDIENT

- ➢ 90 g almond flour
- ➢ 1 egg (size M)
- ➢ 40 g erythritol
- ➢ 65 g soft butter
- ➢ 250 g unsweetened almond milk
- ➢ 100 g erythritol
- ➢ 2 egg yolks
- ➢ 1/2 teaspoon guar gum
- ➢ 5 drops of natural vanilla flavor
- ➢ A 4 cm springform pan
- ➢ A cake ring

> Muffin tins

PREPARATION

Preheat the oven to 175 ° C with a fan oven.

Mix all the ingredients for the batter in a bowl.

Use your hands to knead the dough into a solid mass.

Roll out the dough thinly and prick or cut out 10 cm circles.

Press the batter into the greased cupcake liners and prick it several times with a fork.

Mix all ingredients together and heat them in a small saucepan so that the erythritol dissolves.

Spread the pudding mixture in the molds and bake for 25-30 minutes until it is lightly brown.

LOW CARB & KETO BISCUIT CHOCOLATE STICKS

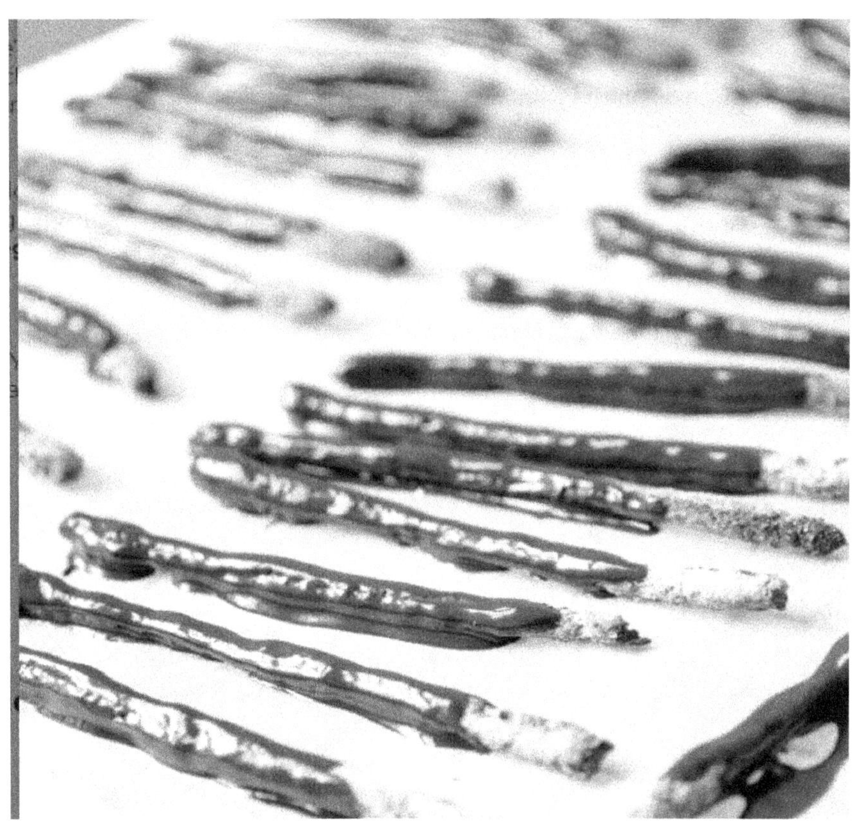

INGREDIENT

- ➢ 50 g almond flour
- ➢ 20 g of crushed flaxseed
- ➢ 10 g psyllium husk powder
- ➢ 150 g warm almond milk
- ➢ 6 g dry yeast (+ 1 pinch of sugar)
- ➢ 10 g powder erythritol
- ➢ 50 g sugar-free chocolate drops

PREPARATION

Warm the almond milk and add the dry yeast with the sugar.

Let the mixture rise for about 15 minutes.

In the meantime, stir all of the remaining ingredients together.

Stir in the yeast milk.

Mix everything into a homogeneous mass and let it swell for about 15 minutes.

Roll out the dough about 0.5 cm thick and cut it into thin strips.

Place the strips of dough on a baking sheet lined with baking paper and bake for about 20 minutes at 180 ° C.

Let the raw sticks cool down and cover with melted chocolate.

LOW-CARB CAULIFLOWER RICE BOWL WITH CHICKEN TERIYAKI

INGREDIENT

- ➢ 1 pack of Full Green cauliflower rice
- ➢ For the chicken:
- ➢ 250 g chicken breast fillet
- ➢ 1 teaspoon coconut oil
- ➢ 2 tbsp soy sauce
- ➢ 2 tbsp water
- ➢ 1 teaspoon guar gum
- ➢ Salt pepper
- ➢ 1/2 teaspoon erythritol
- ➢ Magic Chicken Seasoning
- ➢ toasted sesame seeds
- ➢ 1 spring onion
- ➢ Vegetables at will, e.g. B. Broccoli

PREPARATION

Cut the chicken into bite-sized pieces and sauté them with coconut oil in a large pan.

When the chicken is done, deglaze it with soy sauce and water.

Thicken the sauce with guar gum and season everything with chicken, salt and pepper.

Cut the broccoli into florets and fry them in a pan until they are firm to the bite.

Prepare the rice in the microwave or pan according to the instructions on the packet.

Arrange everything in a bowl and garnish the bowl with sesame seeds and spring onion rings.

KETO PIZZA SNAIL

INGREDIENT

- ➢ 1/2 pack pizza baking mix
- ➢ 200g water
- ➢ 10g olive oil
- ➢ 50g tomato puree
- ➢ 1/2 teaspoon Italian herbs
- ➢ Salt pepper
- ➢ 75g grated mozzarella
- ➢ 100g vegetables of your choice (mushrooms, onions, broccoli)
- ➢ 50g salami or ham

PREPARATION

In a small saucepan, heat the tomato puree with herbs and spices and simmer for about 10 minutes, until the sauce has thickened a little.

In the meantime, cut the vegetables and sausage into small pieces.

Put the pizza baking mixture in a mixing bowl (remove 2 teaspoons of the mixture), mix with water and olive oil and knead into a smooth dough.

Sprinkle the teaspoons of dry baking mixture on a piece of baking paper. Shape the dough into a ball and roll it out into a circle on the baking paper.

Spread about 3/4 of the tomato sauce on the dough and put the chopped ingredients on the dough.

Roll up the dough and cut into slices about 2 cm thick.

Place the rolls in a greased casserole dish and bake in the oven for about 35 minutes at 175 ° C until the surface is nice and brown.

Then sprinkle the pre-baked pizza rolls with grated mozzarella and bake for another 10 minutes until the cheese has melted.

HEARTY KETO EASTER CAKE WITH SALMON CREAM

INGREDIENT

- ➢ 1 pack of Simply Keto "light baking mix"
- ➢ 500g water
- ➢ 40g apple cider vinegar
- ➢ 150g smoked salmon
- ➢ 200g cream cheese
- ➢ 100g Greek yogurt
- ➢ 50g fresh cucumber
- ➢ Fresh dill
- ➢ Salt pepper
- ➢ 100g radishes
- ➢ 200g cream cheese
- ➢ 100g Greek yogurt

- ➢ 1 hard-boiled egg
- ➢ Salt pepper
- ➢ Fresh chives
- ➢ 1 bunch of chives, hard-boiled eggs, cherry tomatoes, and radish-fresh herbs such as basil, cress or parsley

PREPARATION

Put the light baking mixture with hot water and apple cider vinegar in a large mixing bowl and mix everything into a homogeneous batter.

Spread the dough in a greased springform pan and bake it at 175 ° C for 50 minutes until it is golden brown.

Let the soil cool down completely.

Cut the smoked salmon into small cubes.

Halve the cucumber, remove the watery inside with a teaspoon and cut the remaining cucumber into small pieces.

Mix the cream cheese with yoghurt and fold in the finely chopped ingredients.

Season to taste with chopped dill, salt & pepper.

Remove the shell of the boiled egg and dice.

Grate the radishes and mix with the rest of the ingredients. Season to taste here as well.

Cut the cooled bread twice horizontally and place the base on a cake plate.

Now brush half of the radish cream and carefully place the middle base on top.

Now spread the salmon filling on top and put on the top bottom.

Spread the rest of the chives cream all over the bread cake.

Let the hearty cake stand in the refrigerator for 60 minutes.

Remove the shell from the boiled eggs and cut in half.

Halve the cherry tomatoes as well.

Cut the radishes into thin slices.

Decorate the edge of the cake with chives.

Decorate the top with egg and tomato halves, radish slices and cress.

KETO CREAM AND FOREST BERRY CAKE WITH PISTACHIOS

INGREDIENT

- ➢ 1/4 pack Kuchenglück baking mix
- ➢ 100 g of water
- ➢ 500 ml whipped cream
- ➢ 40 g powder erythritol
- ➢ 8 sheets of gelatin
- ➢ 10 drops of vanilla flavor
- ➢ 2 tbsp Simply Keto wild berry jam
- ➢ 1 tbsp pistachios
- ➢ Fresh strawberries
- ➢ A smaller, round 18 cm cake pan and a cake ring

PREPARATION

Mix the quarter pack of Kuchenglück baking mix with water according to the instructions on the packaging.

Put the dough in a round baking pan and bake it for 30 - 35 minutes at 175 ° C fan oven.

Then let the soil cool down completely.

Soak the gelatin in cold water for about 5 minutes.

Now whip the whipped cream until stiff.

Mix in the powdered erythritol and vanilla flavor.

Pour off the water from the gelatin and slowly pour the gelatin into the cream mixture, stirring constantly

Place the bottom shelf on a flat surface and place the cake ring around it.

Spread 1/4 of the cream on top.

Put some strawberry jam on top of the cream.

Spread the rest of the cream on top.

Decorate the cake with pistachios and strawberries as you like.

Put the cake in the cold for at least 4 hours before serving.

KETO GRANOLA TARTLETS WITH CHEESECAKE CREAM

INGREDIENT

- ➢ 100 - 120 g salt caramel crunchy muesli
- ➢ 75 g butter
- ➢ 200 g creme fraiche
- ➢ 200 g cream cheese (room temperature)
- ➢ 120 g butter (room temperature)
- ➢ 1/2 lemon
- ➢ 50 g powder erythritol
- ➢ 5 - 10 drops of natural vanilla flavor

PREPARATION

Melt the butter in the microwave.

Put the granola in a blender and blend it finely.

Mix it with the melted butter to form a homogeneous batter.

Put the batter in muffin cups or small dessert rings and press firmly.

Chill the floors until you are ready to use them.

Mix all ingredients with a hand mixer or in a stand mixer until you get a creamy, fluffy mixture.

Spread the cream on the muffin cups and put the muesli tartlets in the fridge for about 45 minutes.

KETO QUICHE LORRAINE

INGREDIENT

- 85 g almond flour
- 40 g coconut flour
- 1 teaspoon psyllium husk powder
- 1 egg
- 60 ml of cold water
- 2 tbsp olive oil
- For the filling:
- 1 small onion
- 1/2 stick of leek
- 75 g bacon
- 125 g whipped cream
- 2 eggs
- 50 g mountain cheese

   ➢ Some grated nutmeg
   ➢ Salt pepper

PREPARATION

Put all ingredients in a mixing bowl and knead until a homogeneous dough is formed.

Wrap it in cling film and chill for 10 minutes.

Then roll out the dough about 0.5 cm thick with a rolling pin. TIP: If you put cling film on the dough, the rolling pin won't stick to it!

Place the rolled-out dough in a greased springform pan.

Blind prebake the dough at 180 ° C top and bottom heat for 10 minutes.

In the meantime, peel the onion and cut into cubes.

Cut the leek lengthways, wash thoroughly and cut into rings.

Cut the bacon into cubes.

Fry the bacon in a large pan without adding any fat.

Then add the leek rings and onion cubes and fry in them until translucent.

Whisk eggs and whipped cream together in a mixing bowl.

Roughly grate the mountain cheese and add to the egg mixture together with the fried vegetables and mix everything together. Season with salt, pepper and grated nutmeg.

Spread the filling on the baked base and bake the quiche for another 30 to 35 minutes.

Then let cool down a bit, remove from the mold, cut into pieces and enjoy.

KETO CURD BUNNIES

INGREDIENT

- ➢ 100 g quark
- ➢ 50 g coconut oil
- ➢ 110 g almond milk without sugar
- ➢ 3 drops of vanilla flavor
- ➢ 1 egg
- ➢ 10 g psyllium husks
- ➢ 50 g erythritol
- ➢ 200 g almond flour
- ➢ 2 teaspoons of baking soda
- ➢ 50 g of liquid butter
- ➢ 30 g erythritol

PREPARATION

Melt the coconut oil and let it cool down briefly.

Mix the quark, coconut oil, almond milk, vanilla flavor and the egg together in a bowl.

Next, mix the dry ingredients together.

Now slowly sift the dry ingredients into the quark mass and stir with a whisk until a homogeneous mass is formed. If the dough is still too firm, add some almond milk.

Let the dough rest for about 20 minutes.

Roll out the dough so that it is approx. 1 cm thick and cut it out with molds as desired.

Brush the pieces of dough with a little butter.

Preheat the oven to 180 ° convection.

Now place it on a baking sheet lined with baking paper and bake it for about 15 minutes until it is golden-brown.

Take out of the oven, brush with butter again and roll in erythritol.

Then let cool a little on a wire rack and enjoy fresh.

LOW CARB & KETO WEBSITE LAUNCH PIE

INGREDIENT

- ➢ 1 egg
- ➢ 50 g powder erythritol
- ➢ 50 g butter
- ➢ 25 g ground almonds
- ➢ 75 g almond flour
- ➢ 1/2 teaspoon psyllium husks
- ➢ 1/4 teaspoon baking powder
- ➢ For the chocolate base layer:
- ➢ 175 g sugar-free chocolate drops
- ➢ 75 g coconut oil
- ➢ 100 g whipped cream

- ➢ For the biscuit intermediate layer:
- ➢ 25 g baking cocoa
- ➢ 4 eggs
- ➢ 80 g erythritol
- ➢ 25 g almond flour
- ➢ 25 g ground almonds
- ➢ 600 g whipped cream
- ➢ 6 sheets of gelatin
- ➢ 120 g powder erythritol
- ➢ 150 g sugar-free whole milk chocolate drops
- ➢ For the chocolate icing:
- ➢ 120 g whipped cream
- ➢ 100 g sugar-free whole milk chocolate drops

PREPARATION

First, melt the butter in the microwave or in a small saucepan.

Now put all the ingredients for the dough in a mixing bowl and mix everything until a homogeneous mass is formed.

Place the dough in the refrigerator for 10 minutes.

Sprinkle the work surface with a little almond flour and roll out the dough with a rolling pin evenly about 0.5 - 1 cm thick.

Use a sharp knife to cut the dough into rectangular pieces, the shape is not so important as it will crumble the biscuits.

Bake the biscuits at 175 ° C for 10 minutes until golden brown and then let them cool down.

Gently melt the chocolate and coconut oil in a double boiler or microwave.

Add the cream and beat the mixture with a whisk until creamy.

Roughly crumble 200 g of the biscuits, stir everything together and pour the mixture into a round springform pan or a cake ring (24 cm) and refrigerate the base.

Beat the eggs with erythritol for about 5 minutes until frothy.

Mix the remaining ingredients together and fold them into the egg mixture.

Put the dough in a greased 18 cm baking pan and bake the base for about 15 minutes until golden brown.

Then let the soil cool down.

Gently melt the chocolate in a double boiler.

Now whip half of the whipped cream with the powdered erythritol until stiff.

Pour the other half of the cream into the chocolate and stir until it becomes a creamy mass.

Now add the chocolate mass to the whipped cream and stir everything together.

Soak the gelatin sheets in cold water for 5 minutes. Take out the softened gelatin and dissolve it with a small splash of water. Make sure that it never boils!

Pour the liquid gelatine slowly into the chocolate and cream mixture, stirring constantly with the food processor or mixer.

Now spread half of the chocolate mousse on the cake base, carefully place the sponge cake base on top and distribute the rest of the mousse on the intermediate base.

Put the cake in the cold for 1 hour.

Melt the chocolate with about 50 grams of heavy cream.

Then stir in the rest of the cream with a whisk.

Now carefully remove the cake ring. If the cream is not yet set, put the cake ring around it again and put it in the cold again.

Now spread the chocolate icing over the cake and put it in the cold until serving.

You can decorate them with gold leaf, gold paint and chocolate rasps if you like.

KETO RISOTTO WITH GREEN ASPARAGUS

INGREDIENT

- ➢ 300 g green asparagus
- ➢ 140 g konja circle
- ➢ 1 L vegetable stock
- ➢ 40 g pine nuts
- ➢ Butter
- ➢ For the parmesan cream:
- ➢ 75 g butter
- ➢ 2 cloves of garlic
- ➢ 120 g cream cheese
- ➢ 110 ml of heavy cream
- ➢ 120 ml unsweetened almond milk
- ➢ 55 g parmesan cheese
- ➢ 2 teaspoons of oregano
- ➢ Salt pepper

- ➢ For the pesto:
- ➢ 5 tbsp pine nuts
- ➢ 5 handfuls of basil leaves
- ➢ 8 tbsp parmesan
- ➢ 2 cloves of garlic
- ➢ 1/2 lemon
- ➢ 80 ml of olive oil
- ➢ Salt pepper

PREPARATION

For the beginning

Let the rice simmer in the vegetable stock for 15 minutes, stirring again and again.

Cut away the bottom ends of the asparagus.

Cut the asparagus into smaller pieces and boil in the water for 10 minutes.

Put all ingredients in a small saucepan and let everything soften over medium heat.

As soon as a homogeneous mass is formed, stir well again and again so that there are no more lumps.

Season to taste.

Put all ingredients in a blender and hex until you get a homogeneous mass.

Season to taste.

Fry the pine nuts in a little butter.

Drain the rice and mix with the Parmesan cream, asparagus and pine nuts. Let simmer again briefly.

When serving, like to refine with basil leaves and the pesto.

KETO DOME CAKE WITH TWO DIFFERENT FILLINGS

INGREDIENT

- ➢ 1/2 pack Kuchenglück baking mix
- ➢ 100 g of water
- ➢ For the white dome inside:
- ➢ 80 g yogurt (3.5% fat)
- ➢ 20 g lemon juice
- ➢ 100 g whipped cream
- ➢ 4 sheets of gelatin
- ➢ 4 drops of natural vanilla flavor
- ➢ For the berry cream:
- ➢ 150 g wild berries
- ➢ 250 g quark (40% fat)
- ➢ 250 g whipped cream
- ➢ 40 g erythritol
- ➢ 6 sheets of gelatin
- ➢ Fresh berries for decoration

> 18 cm springform pan

PREPARATION

Mix half of the Kuchenglück baking mix with water and pour into a greased 18 cm springform pan.

Bake according to the instructions and let cool down completely.

Soak gelatine in cold water.

Mix the cream with the vanilla flavor and whip until stiff.

Squeeze out the soaked gelatine, heat it briefly in a small saucepan or in the microwave and then let it cool down.

Carefully stir the liquid gelatine into the stiff cream in portions.

Whip the yogurt together with the lemon juice in a separate bowl until creamy.

Now stir both masses together.

Pour the mixture into a round container lined with cling film (e.g., cereal bowl) and put in the refrigerator for about 20 minutes.

Simmer the berries in a small saucepan for about 5 minutes.

Then pass through a sieve.

Soak gelatine in cold water and then heat it briefly until it liquefies.

Beat the cream together with the erythritol until stiff.

Add the quark and the berry juice to the cream mixture.

Carefully stir the liquid gelatine into the stiff cream in portions.

Put the cake ring around the cake base and place the firm cream upside down on it.

Carefully spread the berry cream over it so that the hemisphere is completely covered.

Let the cake set in the refrigerator for about 20 minutes.

Decorate with fresh berries as desired and enjoy.

KETO MINI WALBERRY TARTLETS WITH MERINGUE

INGREDIENT

- 90 g almond flour
- 1 egg (size M)
- 40 g erythritol
- 65 g butter (room temperature)
- 100 g mascapone
- 1 egg
- 20 g erythritol
- 5 drops of natural vanilla flavor
- 1 pinch of locust bean gum
- 20 g cream
- Sugar-free Simply Keto wild berry fruit spread
- 50 ml of water
- 200 g erythritol
- 2 egg whites
- pinch of salt

PREPARATION

Preheat the oven to 175 ° C with a fan oven.

Mix all the ingredients for the batter in a bowl.

Use your hands to knead the dough into a solid mass.

Dust the dough with enough bamboo flour and roll it out between two layers of cling film.

Now press the dough into the greased form, prick it several times with a fork and bake it for 8-10 minutes until it is lightly brown.

Then let cool down completely.

Mix the mascarpone with the egg, erythritol, cream and vanilla flavor to a homogeneous mixture.

Pour the filling into the prepared tartlet molds and bake for 24-26 minutes.

Take out and let cool on a wire rack.

Spread some wild berry fruit spread on the filling.

Mix the water with 150 g of the erythritol in a small saucepan and let it simmer.

As soon as the erythritol has dissolved, remove the syrup from the stove and let it cool down a little.

Beat the egg white with a pinch of salt until it hardens.

Slowly mix in the rest of the erythritol and continue to beat until stiff.

Meanwhile, carefully mix the erythritol syrup into the egg white mass and continue whipping until a firm and shiny meringue is formed.

Pour the mixture into a piping bag and sprinkle small dots on the tartlets.

Either flambé the meringue or lightly brown it in the oven for about 5 minutes using the grill function.

KETO MOCHA CREAM SANDWICHES

INGREDIENT

- ➢ 1 pack of Simply Keto Cake Mix
- ➢ 240 g butter (room temperature)
- ➢ 300 g cream cheese (room temperature)
- ➢ 60 g powder erythritol
- ➢ 4 tsp instant coffee powder
- ➢ 150 g whipped cream
- ➢ 100 g sugar-free dark chocolate drops
- ➢ 20 g powder erythritol
- ➢ A 20 x 20 brownie baking pan

PREPARATION

Prepare the soil according to the instructions on the package.

Let the soil cool off well.

Beat the butter and cream cheese until frothy (important: both must be at room temperature) and then sieve in the powdered erythritol and the coffee powder.

Halve the cake so that there are two cake bases.

Spread half of the cream on the first floor.

Melt the chocolate drops with about 50 g of cream.

When the chocolate is melted, sieve the powdered erythritol into the chocolate.

Then stir in the rest of the cream with a whisk until a thick mixture is formed.

Pour the ganache on the cream layer and put it in the fridge for at least an hour.

Now put the second floor on top and coat the top with the cream again.

Pour another layer of chocolate ganache on top and let it dry again.

KETO YEAST DUMPLINGS WITH PLUM FILLING

INGREDIENT

- ➢ 75ml warm water
- ➢ 2 tsp dry yeast (half a packet)
- ➢ 1/2 teaspoon sugar
- ➢ 30g bamboo flour (available here)
- ➢ 10g psyllium husk flour (available here)
- ➢ 20g ground almonds
- ➢ 25g erythritol (available here)
- ➢ 1 egg
- ➢ 50g quark (40% fat)
- ➢ 20g soft butter
- ➢ For the filling
- ➢ 1 plum
- ➢ 1/2 tbsp erythritol (available here)
- ➢ Some water

PREPARATION

Mix the water, yeast and sugar together and leave to rest in a warm place for about 10 minutes.

Mix the egg, quark, butter and erythritol until you get a homogeneous mixture

Mix the flour and almonds and add to the dough alternately with the yeast mixture and stir in.

Core the plum and cut into small pieces.

Simmer in a small saucepan with 1/2 tbsp erythritol and some water over medium heat for a few minutes until the plums disintegrate.

Shape the dough into 2-3 balls and set aside some of the dough.

Press a hole in the center of the balls with your finger.

Fill the plums into the hole and seal the opening with the rest of the batter.

Let the balls rise in a warm place for at least 1 hour.

Cook over a water bath in steam for 30 minutes.

CHOCOLATE KETO TARTLETS WITH BERRIES

INGREDIENT

- ➢ 90g almond flour (available here)
- ➢ 5g baking cocoa
- ➢ 1 egg (size M)
- ➢ 40g erythritol (available here)
- ➢ 65g soft butter
- ➢ 50g Simply Keto chocolate (available here)
- ➢ 50g whipped cream
- ➢ A handful of fresh berries
- ➢ 4 tartlet molds

PREPARATION

Preheat the oven to 175 ° C with a fan oven.

Mix all the ingredients for the batter in a bowl.

Use your hands to knead the dough into a solid mass.

Press the dough in portions into the greased molds, prick it several times with a fork and bake it for 8-10 minutes until it is lightly brown.

Then let the soil cool down completely.

Gently melt the chocolate together with the whipped cream in a small saucepan.

Fill the chocolate filling evenly into the tart molds and put them in the cold for at least 1 hour until the filling is firm.

Decorate the tartlets with fresh berries, chopped chocolate pieces or desiccated coconut as you wish.

BERRY CREAM

INGREDIENT

- ➤ 100 - 120g cinnamon crunchy muesli
- ➤ 75g butter
- ➤ For the cream
- ➤ 100g fresh fruits (e.g., blueberries, raspberries, strawberries)
- ➤ 25g Simply Keto wild berry jam (available here)
- ➤ 35g powder erythritol (available here)
- ➤ 90ml whipped cream
- ➤ 3 sheets of gelatin

PREPARATION

Melt the butter in the microwave.

Put the granola in a blender and blend it finely.

Mix it with the melted butter to form a homogeneous batter.

Put the batter in muffin cups or small dessert rings and press firmly.

Chill the floors until you are ready to use them.

Soak the gelatin sheets in cold water for about 5 minutes.

Puree the fruit and then stir together the powdered erythritol and jam in it.

Whip the whipped cream until stiff and fold in the berry mixture.

Take the gelatin out of the water and let it drain a little. Gently dissolve the gelatin in a small saucepan or in the microwave. Make sure it doesn't boil!

Now pour the gelatin into the bowl with the cream mixture, stirring constantly.

Let the mixture set in the refrigerator or freezer until it has the consistency of easy-to-spread cream cheese.

Now spread the pudding cream on the cooled muesli bases and let them cool down.

<u>FILLED KETO PEPPERS – VEGETARIAN</u>

INGREDIENT

- ➢ 2 peppers (or vegetables of your choice, e.g., zuccini, aubergine)
- ➢ 1 small onion
- ➢ 1 clove of garlic
- ➢ 1 pack of rice from Palmini
- ➢ 1 can of pureed tomatoes
- ➢ a pinch of salt and pepper
- ➢ fresh herbs of your choice (e.g., parsley, basil)

PREPARATION

Rinse the rice from Palmini made from palm hearts in a fine sieve with cold water and allow to drain.

Halve the peppers (or vegetables of your choice) or cut off the lid and core.

Then rub with olive oil and prebake in the oven for 5-10 minutes.

Peel the onion and garlic and cut into small cubes, sauté.

Mix onion cubes and garlic with tomato sauce and fresh herbs of your choice and simmer.

Take the peppers (or vegetables of your choice) out of the oven and fill with the prepared filling.

Optionally top with feta cheese.

Bake the whole thing for about 15-20 minutes on the middle rack in the oven at 175 ° C, until the feta cheese is golden brown.

Optionally refine with the rest of the fresh herbs.

KETO SPAGHETTI ALLA PUTTANESCA

INGREDIENT

- ➢ 1 can of Palmini Angel Hair Spaghetti
- ➢ For the sauce
- ➢ 120g small sardines in olive oil
- ➢ 1 clove of garlic
- ➢ 60g black olives
- ➢ 400g tomato puree
- ➢ 2 tbsp capers
- ➢ 1 fresh chilli
- ➢ 2 tbsp olive oil
- ➢ Salt pepper

PREPARATION

Peel and finely chop the garlic.

Core the chilli and cut into small cubes.

Cut the olives into slices if necessary.

Cut the sardine fillets into small pieces.

In a small saucepan, sauté the chopped garlic, olive rings and chili cubes in olive oil.

Add the chopped tomatoes and simmer for about 10 minutes at a low temperature.

Add capers and sardine fillets and season with salt and pepper.

Rinse off Palmini Angel Hair and add to the saucepan with the tomato sauce and heat.

Spread the pasta alla puttanesca on a plate and enjoy.

Reviews

KETO BROWNIE MUFFINS WITH RASPBERRY FILLING

INGREDIENT

- ➢ 1/2 pack of Simply Keto Bownie Baking Mix
- ➢ 80g fresh raspberries
- ➢ 25g powder erythritol
- ➢ 100ml whipped cream
- ➢ 1 sheet of gelatin
- ➢ 2 drops of sugar-free vanilla flavor
- ➢

PREPARATION

Prepare half of the brownie baking mixture according to the instructions, fill the dough into muffin molds, bake for about 15 minutes and then leave to cool.

Scoop out the muffins with the help of a teaspoon.

Soak the gelatine in cold water for about 5 minutes.

Heat the raspberries together with powdered erythritol and bring to the boil briefly. (If desired, remove the cores using a sieve).

Take the gelatine out of the water and let it drain.

Carefully dissolve the gelatin in the raspberry-erythritol mixture by continuing to heat the mixture, but not boiling it. Mix well!

Whip the cream together with the vanilla flavoring until stiff.

Carefully fold the raspberry gelatine mixture into the cream.

Now fill the muffins - it's easier with a piping bag, but a teaspoon does it too.

Decorate with raspberries and chill.

KETO LEMON AND ALMOND CAKE WITHOUT BAKING MIX

INGREDIENT

- ➢ 6 eggs
- ➢ 230 g erythritol
- ➢ 200 g coconut oil
- ➢ 400 g ground almonds
- ➢ 50 g coconut flour
- ➢ 1 teaspoon Baking powder
- ➢ Juice and zest of 1 lemon
- ➢ For the frosting:
- ➢ 1 lemon
- ➢ 130 g powder erythritol

PREPARATION

First, melt the coconut oil. Rub the zest of the lemon and extract the juice.

Now put all the ingredients in a bowl and stir them until you have a homogeneous mass.

Now spread the dough in a square, greased baking pan.

Now bake the cake for about 80 minutes at 170 ° C top / bottom heat (every oven is a bit different, so watch the cake after 60 minutes and take it out as soon as it starts to get dark).

Let the cake cool for 1 hour before removing it from the pan.

Mix the lemon juice well with the powdered erythritol, making sure that no lumps are visible in the mass.

TIP: If the frosting is too runny, add more powdered erythritol. If it's too thick, add more lemon juice.

Now carefully pour the frosting over the completely cooled cake.

TIP: If you want a thicker frosting, let the first layer dry and repeat the process.

KETO CALZONES

INGREDIENT

- ➢ 1/2 pack of pizza baking mix
- ➢ 200g water
- ➢ 10g olive oil
- ➢ For the tomato sauce
- ➢ 50g tomato puree
- ➢ 1/2 teaspoon Italian herbs
- ➢ Salt pepper
- ➢ For the filling
- ➢ 75g grated mozzarella
- ➢ 100g vegetables of your choice (mushrooms, onions, broccoli)
- ➢ 50g salami or ham

PREPARATION

In a small saucepan, heat the tomato puree with herbs and spices and simmer for about 10 minutes, until the sauce has thickened a little.

In the meantime, cut the vegetables and sausage into small pieces.

Put the pizza baking mixture in a mixing bowl (remove 2 teaspoons of the mixture), mix with water and olive oil and knead into a smooth dough.

Sprinkle the teaspoons of dry baking mixture on a piece of baking paper. Shape the dough into a ball and roll it out into a circle on the baking paper.

Spread the tomato sauce on the dough and place the chopped ingredients on one half of the dough.

Sprinkle the grated mozzarella on top and fold the dough over.

Press the edge into place, either with a fork or with your hands.

Spread some tomato sauce and cheese on top if you like.

Bake the calzone in the oven for 40 minutes at 175 ° C until the surface is nice and brown.

LOW CARB & KETO BROWNIE LAYER DESSERT

INGREDIENT

- 100ml whipped cream
- For the brownie layer
- 1/2 pack of Simply Keto Bownie Baking Mix
- Butter & water for the baking mix
- For the chocolate mousse layer
- 100ml whipped cream
- 40g sugar-free dark chocolate drops

PREPARATION

Prepare the baking mixture according to the instructions and let it cool down completely.

Put 50 g whipped cream and the chocolate drops in a small saucepan and heat carefully until the chocolate has melted.

Whip the remaining cold cream (50 g) until stiff.

Carefully fold in the stiff cream and let the mousse set in the refrigerator.

Whip the cream until stiff and set aside.

Spread a thin layer of chocolate mousse on the bottom of each container.

Spread some cream on top.

Crumble the brownie and sprinkle on the mousse.

Now fill the vessels with alternating layers and top with brownie crumbs.

KETO ALMOND CAKE WITHOUT BAKING MIX

INGREDIENT

- ➢ 200g almond flour
- ➢ 4 eggs
- ➢ 1 teaspoon lemon zest
- ➢ 30g sliced almonds
- ➢ 40g erythritol
- ➢ Some powder erythritol
- ➢ Some sugar-free sour cherry fruit spread

PREPARATION

Preheat the oven to 180 ° C fan-assisted.

Separate the yolks from the whites.

Mix the almond flour, erythritol, lemon zest and egg yolks together.

Beat the separated egg whites until stiff and carefully fold them into the almond flour mixture.

Pour the dough into a greased or parchment-lined mold, spread the almond slivers on the cake and bake it for 40 minutes until the edges turn golden brown.

Optional: Let the cake cool for 15 minutes, sprinkle it with powdered erythritol and enjoy it with some of our sour cherry fruit spread.

COLORFUL SPRINKLES - NO SUGAR!

INGREDIENT

- 85g powder erythritol
- 1 egg white
- 5 drops of natural vanilla flavor
- Sugar-free food color at will

PREPARATION

Put the egg whites in a mixing bowl and beat very stiffly.

Then add the powdered erythritol in portions and the vanilla flavor and beat the mixture again.

Depending on the number of colors, divide the mixture, divide it into small bowls and stir in the food coloring. Start with 3 drops and check the result.

Fill the prepared crumble mixture into freezer bags or prepared piping nozzles and apply in long lines on baking paper.

Let the streusel dry for several hours, preferably overnight.

Finally break into small sprinkles with your hands.

TIP: The sprinkles go well with cake pops

KETO BREADED SCHNITZEL

INGREDIENT

- ➢ 2 schnitzel (pork or poultry as you like)
- ➢ 2 eggs
- ➢ 30 g almond flour
- ➢ 50 g pork crust chips
- ➢ Salt pepper
- ➢ Coconut oil for frying

PREPARATION

Wash the meat thoroughly and pat dry with a kitchen towel.

Then season it with salt and pepper.

Put the pork crust chips in a blender and puree them finely.

Put the almond flour and the crushed chips in a bowl.

Whisk the egg in a second bowl.

First roll the meat in the almond flour, then dip it in the egg and then roll it in the crushed chips.

Heat a coated pan and generously add coconut oil for frying.

Carefully add the breaded schnitzel and fry for 5 - 8 minutes on each side over low heat.

KETO FETA PASTA

INGREDIENT

- ➢ 1 can of Palmini Spaghetti
- ➢ 200g feta
- ➢ 300g cherry tomatoes
- ➢ 3 cloves of garlic
- ➢ Fresh or dried herbs (basil, parsley, oregano)
- ➢ 3 tbsp olive oil
- ➢ Salt pepper

PREPARATION

Place the cherry tomatoes in a baking dish until the bottom is completely covered.

Put the feta in the middle and drizzle everything with olive oil.

Peel and chop the garlic.

Also chop the fresh herbs and place in the baking dish with salt and pepper.

Bake everything in the oven at 175 ° C for 30 - 40 minutes.

Then take the mold out of the oven and mix everything together, including the feta.

Finally, heat the Palmini pasta and mix in the middle of the rest of the ingredients.

Arrange on plates and enjoy.

KETO VALENTINE'S DAY PIE WITH BERRY FILLING

INGREDIENT

- ➤ 90g almond flour
- ➤ 1 egg (size M)
- ➤ 40g erythritol
- ➤ 65g warm butter
- ➤ 100g fresh fruits (e.g., blueberries, raspberries, strawberries)
- ➤ 25g Oh! Delicious strawberry-raspberry jam
- ➤ 65g powder erythritol
- ➤ 90ml whipped cream
- ➤ 1 egg

PREPARATION

Preheat the oven to 175 ° C with a fan oven.

Mix all the ingredients for the batter in a mixing bowl.

Use your hands to knead the dough into a firm shortcrust pastry mass.

Dust the dough with a little almond flour and roll out the dough (if necessary, between two layers of cling film).

Now press half of the dough into the greased tart pan. The edge of the dough should be about 1 - 2 cm high.

Use a cookie cutter to cut hearts out of the rest of the dough.

Sieve the powdered erythritol so that there are no lumps in the filling later.

Mix all the ingredients together and pour the mixture into the tart pan.

Now place the punched-out dough hearts on the edge and on the filling.

Bake the pie for 30-35 minutes, until it is light brown and firm.

<u>KETO TIGER DONUTS</u>

INGREDIENT

- ➢ 2 eggs
- ➢ 75 g erythritol
- ➢ 65 g butter
- ➢ 115 g blanched & ground almonds
- ➢ 15 g bamboo flour
- ➢ 1/3 teaspoon baking powder
- ➢ 50 g sugar-free dark chocolate

PREPARATION

First, melt the butter.

Now put all the ingredients (except the chocolate) in a bowl and stir them until you have a homogeneous mass.

Finely chop the chocolate.

Finally, carefully fold in the chopped chocolate.

Now spread the batter into the silicone donut baking pan.

Bake the donuts for 15 minutes at 170 ° C top / bottom heat.

Now let the donuts cool before removing them from the mold.

Decorate the donuts with liquid chocolate.

LOW CARB & KETO BLUEBERRY SWIRL CAKE

INGREDIENT

- ➢ 1 pack of keto cake mix
- ➢ 260g water
- ➢ 50g sugar-free chocolate
- ➢ 350ml cream
- ➢ 4 sheets of gelatin
- ➢ 40g powder erythritol
- ➢ 200g berries / fruits as desired

PREPARATION

In a large mixing bowl, knead the cake mix with water.

Gently melt the sugar-free chocolate and mix it into the batter.

Put the chocolate dough in a round (greased) springform pan and bake it for about 30 minutes at 175 ° C.

Let it cool completely before cutting it.

Now halve the baked cake base horizontally with a long knife and place one half in a cake ring.

Puree the berries and strain them through a sieve if necessary.

Soak the gelatine sheets in cold water for about 5 minutes. Now whip the cream until stiff.

 Sieve the powdered erythritol through a sieve to avoid leaving lumps in the cream mixture. Add the powdered erythritol to the whipped cream and mix everything again vigorously. Now pour off the water from the gelatine and let the gelatine leaves drip off a little.

Now carefully melt this until it dissolves completely. Make sure she's not boiling!

Pour the gelatine slowly into the cream, stirring constantly.

Spread the cream mixture on the cake base and use a tablespoon to pour the pureed fruit onto the cream in blobs. Fold in the blobs of berries loosely so that a marbling appears.

Place the second floor on top and press it down lightly.

 Place the chocolate swirl cake in the refrigerator for about an hour and then decorate it with blueberries as you like.

KETO BUNDT CAKE WITH RASPBERRIES

INGREDIENT

- ➤ 6 eggs
- ➤ 230 g erythritol
- ➤ 200 g butter
- ➤ 350 g blanched & ground almonds
- ➤ 50 g bamboo flour
- ➤ 1 teaspoon Baking powder
- ➤ 150 g raspberries (fresh or frozen)
- ➤ 130 - 150 g powder erythritol
- ➤ Juice of 1/2 lemon

PREPARATION

First, melt the butter.

Now put all the ingredients (except the raspberries) in a bowl and stir them until you have a homogeneous mixture.

Finally, carefully fold in the raspberries. TIP: If you use frozen raspberries, it works best.

Now distribute the dough in a silicone baking pan.

Now bake the cake for 60 - 80 minutes at 170 ° C top / bottom heat (every oven is a bit different, so watch the cake after 60 minutes and take it out as soon as it starts to get dark).

Let the cake cool for 1 hour before removing it from the pan.

Mix the powdered erythritol and lemon juice to a smooth glaze.

Brush the Gugelhupf with the lemon glaze and decorate it with fresh raspberries.

KETO CREPES

INGREDIENT

- ➤ 20 g almond flour
- ➤ 3 eggs (size M)
- ➤ 15 g erythritol
- ➤ 50 g cream cheese
- ➤ 1 pinch of salt
- ➤ 30 g butter for frying
- ➤ For the filling:
- ➤ 50 g sugar-free chocolate drops
- ➤ 50 g whipped cream
- ➤ A handful of fresh berries

PREPARATION

In a mixing bowl, beat the eggs until frothy.

Add the cream cheese, almond flour, erythritol and salt and mix everything together thoroughly. Let the crepe dough rest for 5 minutes.

Heat some butter in a large pan and add 3-4 tablespoons of the batter.

Swirl the pan or use a tablespoon to spread the batter evenly across the pan.

Fry the crepes on one side until the edges are lightly browned and gently peel off.

Turn the crepes over and finish baking.

Our favorite food is crêpes with sugar-free chocolate and fresh berries.

KETO CHOCOLATE-NUT PYRAMID

INGREDIENT

- ➢ 1 pack Kuchenglück baking mix
- ➢ 50g sugar-free dark chocolate drops
- ➢ 260ml water
- ➢ For the butter and almond cream
- ➢ 80g sugar-free dark chocolate drops
- ➢ 65g almond butter
- ➢ 40g powder erythritol
- ➢ 100g cream cheese
- ➢ 150g butter
- ➢ 50g chopped almonds
- ➢ also
- ➢ 50g chopped almonds

- ➢ 50g erythritol gold
- ➢ For the chocolate ganache
- ➢ 150g whipped cream
- ➢ 100g sugar-free dark chocolate drops

PREPARATION

Preheat the oven to 175 ° C with a fan oven.

Gently melt the chocolate drops.

Mix the cake mix according to the instructions and mix in the melted chocolate.

Pour the batter into a square baking pan / deep baking sheet and bake it for 20-25 minutes.

Then let the soil cool down completely.

Melt the chocolate drops carefully. | Beat the melted chocolate, butter, cream cheese, powdered erythritol and almond butter in a bowl until it becomes a loose, homogeneous mass and put the cream briefly in the refrigerator. | Then put it in the refrigerator

Cut the bottom into 3 to 4 irregularly sized strips so that when you place them on top of each other, they form a pyramid shape.

Brush the widest base with the buttercream and place the next larger base on top. Do the same with the rest of the ingredients.

If necessary, cut off corners or edges so that a proper elongated pyramid is created.

Brush the surface with the rest of the cream and put the cake in the cold.

In a small pan, roast the chopped almonds with erythritol gold. Then let the brittle cool completely and chop it up.

Melt the chocolate with about 50 g of whipped cream in a small saucepan. | Then stir in the rest of the cream with a whisk until a thick mixture is formed. | Lift the brittle under the ganache and decorate the cake with it.

KETO VEGETABLE QUICHE

INGREDIENT

- 100 g almond flour
- 50 g coconut flour
- 1 teaspoon psyllium husk powder
- 1/2 teaspoon salt
- 1 egg
- 70 ml of cold water
- 2 tbsp olive oil
- 2 zucchini
- 3 - 4 carrots
- 1 clove of garlic
- 200 g sour cream
- 1/2 teaspoon locust bean gum
- 2 eggs
- Salt, pepper and nutmeg to taste
- A round 18 cm springfor

PREPARATION

Put all ingredients in a mixing bowl and knead until a homogeneous dough is formed.

Wrap it in cling film and chill for 10 minutes.

Then roll out the dough about 0.5 cm thick with a rolling pin. TIP: If you put cling film on the dough, the rolling pin won't stick to it!

Place the rolled-out dough in a greased springform pan.

Blind prebake the dough at 180 ° C top and bottom heat for 10 minutes.

In the meantime, thinly slice the carrots and zucchini.

Peel and finely chop the garlic and place in a small bowl.

Put the remaining ingredients for the filling in the small bowl and whisk together well.

Spread half of the cream and egg filling on the baked base.

Place the vegetable strips alternately in a circle on the base and spread the rest of the cream and egg filling over them.

Bake the quiche for another 30 to 35 minutes.

Then let cool down a bit.

FAVORITES